Revised and enlarged edition by

WILLIAM R. VAN DERSAL

Wildlife for America

The story of wildlife conservation

HENRY Z. WALCK, INC. / NEW YORK

333.7 Van Dersal, William R.
V
Wildlife for America; the story of wildlife conservation. Rev. and enl. ed. Walck, 1970
160p. photos.

Further Reading: p.150
An up-dated and expanded ed. with many new photographs and an index.

1. Wild life - Conservation I. Title

This Main Entry catalog card may be reproduced without permission.

ISBN: 0-8098-3090-6
Library of Congress Catalog Card Number: 71-100711
Printed in the United States of America

The original edition of *Wildlife for America* appeared in 1949, jointly written by my late friend and colleague, Edward H. Graham, and myself. Twenty years of progress in the field of wildlife conservation has now made it necessary to revise and enlarge the earlier work considerably.

For many years both Dr. Graham and I worked closely with Ernest G. Holt, who initiated the wildlife and biological work of the U.S. Soil Conservation Service. Many of the ideas in this book came originally from him. He was, in fact, among the pioneers in wildlife habitat work, and in relating wildlife conservation and land use programs. He was certainly among the first to see clearly how land use patterns could be modified for wildlife benefit—and to take effective action to bring this about.

It is highly appropriate therefore, that this book be dedicated

TO ERNEST G. HOLT

one of America's great wildlife conservationists

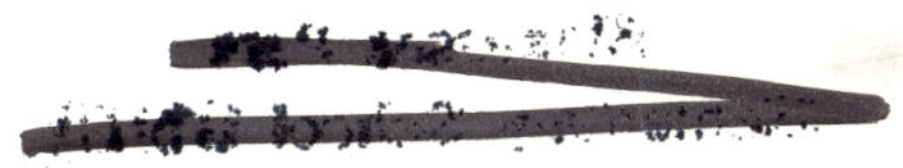

Contents

WILDLIFE NEEDS AND PROBLEMS

WILDLIFE ON THE LAND

PRIMITIVE TIMES

In the beginning—the East

Five hundred years ago wildlife in wonderful abundance could be found everywhere in America.

In the great forest of the East there were white-tailed deer, elk, black bear and wood buffalo. There were grouse, turkeys, passenger pigeons and ivory-billed woodpeckers. In the north woods were timber wolves and moose, lynx and mountain lions, martens, fishers and wolverines. There were myriads of waterfowl and shorebirds, of migratory songbirds, of hawks and owls and a variety of other birds.

Along the Atlantic coast the great auks—penguinlike birds now extinct—ranged from Maine to Florida. With them were numerous seabirds, including the Labrador duck that was found as far south as Chesapeake Bay. Great runs of salmon moved each year from the ocean up the coastal streams and rivers.

In the Central Plains elk, antelope and buffalo ranged in herds comparable to those of the big game populations of Africa. On these vast grasslands there were wolves, coyotes, badgers, jack-rabbits, prairie chickens and sharp-tailed grouse. Millions of prairie dogs occupied the landscape in dog towns, covering dozens or even hundreds of square miles.

In the High Plains along the Rocky Mountains the giant flesh-eating grizzly bear was found in numbers which are hard to grasp today.

A deer in virgin forest

In the beginning—the West

In the towering mountain ranges of the Rockies, west of the Plains, were mountain sheep and goats, mule deer, and ptarmigan. In the interior valleys sage grouse flourished in the pungent sagebrush on which it depended.

Westward in the Sierra Nevada and Cascade Mountains the giant condor, largest of all our birds, sailed and circled. Deer, elk, bear were plentiful, and California quail were to be found in the valleys. Along the Pacific coast, as on the Atlantic, salmon moved up the rivers to spawn and die in incredible numbers each spring.

Far to the southwest peccaries or wild pigs, desert foxes, jaguars and Gila monsters ranged in the desert among cactus and greasewood.

The earliest explorers, trappers, and settlers were astonished at the abundance of game. The journals of those who wrote about what they saw are filled with accounts of "vast numbers," "incredible herds," "birds darkening the sky," "animals as far as the eye could see," and so on.

There was no one to count the numbers of all these animals. Later on, scientists tried to estimate how many there might have been, but no one knows for sure. Some of the wild creatures are gone, some are now very rare, and some have increased. All of them have been affected in one way or another by man.

Prairie dogs of the grasslands

Gila monster of the Southwest

Primitive waterfowl

The wildfowl of our lakes, rivers, and seashores, and of our swamps and marshes existed in numbers far beyond those of today. Ducks, geese, swans and herons were common from east to west. There were avocets, curlews and sandpipers on inland shores, and along the shores of the sea, cormorants, pelicans, gulls, terns and many other curious and wonderful birds were to be seen.

What we have done to water areas has greatly affected wildlife. Once, for example, along the Klamath River of Oregon and California, great flocks of ducks, geese, swans and cranes blotted out the sun. In the marshes there grebes, pelicans, gulls and terns nested by the tens of thousands. Then hunters came who killed the ducks and geese by the wagonloads, to be sold in the city markets for food. Terns and grebes were killed for feathers to decorate ladies' hats. Later, the marshes were drained so the land could be used for growing crops. But much of the land was not good for crops. It became a desert from which clouds of dust arose to shut out the sun, much as the birds had done before.

Now hunters are not allowed to kill waterfowl for sale, and it is against the law to collect wild birds for their feathers. Today we use scientific surveys to find out whether land will be good for crops, before it is drained.

The numbers of waterfowl reached a very low ebb indeed before we began to realize that they might all be exterminated. After several hundred years, we began at last to protect the birds and to set up refuges where they could live and breed.

In early days waterfowl was as common as this

The big game

The big game animals of America existed by the millions in primitive times. Various biologists and naturalists have tried to make the best possible estimates of their numbers, but no one really knows for certain.

Perhaps 10 million elk ranged in our country several centuries ago. There may have been a million moose, most of them in Canada and Alaska, but some in our northern states. Black bear are estimated at half a million, white-tailed deer at 40 million and western mule deer at 10 million. Mountain sheep of our western mountains numbered up to 2 million, mountain goats about half that number.

The really large numbers, of course, were of buffalo and antelope. Ernest Thompson Seton, famous naturalist, believed that there were 30 to 40 million antelope—possibly more—and that the number of buffalo was at least 60 million and possibly 75 million in the United States.

It was the big animals that began to disappear first. They were killed by the early pioneers for food and clothing. Later they were destroyed wholesale for their hides and meat. The bears, the mountain lions and other carnivores were shot to rid the country of their dangerous presence. In the times before the beginning of this century, we very nearly exterminated some of these animals, and we reduced the numbers of all of them to a very tiny fraction of what they once were.

One of America's big game animals—the elk

Exploration

If it had not been for beavers, probably our country would not have been explored as fast as it was. All over America the trappers and traders searched after beaver pelts. The early history of the West is largely a history of the fur trade—and beaver fur was its staple.

Trappers followed closely behind Lewis and Clark. They were ahead of Fremont and the other famous explorers of the Rockies. Some of them lived with the Indians and others fought them. The trappers fought among themselves as well, over rich fur-trading country. They trapped beaver and mink, otter and marten, fox and dozens of other fur animals. The furs brought handsome prices. And so, long before settlers arrived, the trappers had reached almost every corner of our country.

The fur traders began the development of some of our great cities. They started trading posts where the trappers brought their furs to sell. St. Louis was founded by the French traders in 1764, and for a hundred years was one of the great centers of the fur trade. Astoria, founded in 1811 on the Oregon coast, grew up in the same way.

Special hunters were employed by Lewis and Clark and other explorers to supply their expeditions with wild meat for food and skins for clothing.

Little by little the pioneers carved their farms from the wilderness, and gradually they subdued the land. These were the men and women who were building a new nation.

Indians ruled the West when the trappers came

Clearing

As more and more settlers pushed into the wilderness, they cut and burned the trees wholesale. The timber they destroyed would be very valuable today, but in those days it was only in the way. Wherever the land looked as though it might grow food, down came the trees. In order to eat, the settlers had to plow the land and plant their crops.

Westward, on the prairies, the land was good for corn and wheat. There the native grasses grew thickly, shoulder-high in some places. They formed a tough sod that was very difficult to break up and clear away. But the prairie grasses were gradually plowed under. In their place fields of corn and wheat were grown.

With changes like these going on, the creatures of the wild changed too. Many wild animals furnished food as well as clothing for the settlers. Hunters tracked down and killed the cougars, bears and wolves which fed on the settler's livestock and carried off the calves and lambs. The big animals were pushed back as the American wilderness was conquered. There came to be fewer and fewer of them.

The lesser animals, or some of them, fared better. The raccoons took to eating corn. The skunks fed on the insects that came in great variety to plague the crops of the pioneers. Squirrels became fewer as the trees were cut down, but quail increased because they liked the scattered open places mixed with the woods. Songbirds that liked clearings also did better than before. Wildlife populations changed just about as much as the landscape did.

Settlers cleared the forests

The wet land and the dry

After the forests were cut and the prairies plowed, if the land was too wet to farm, the settlers drained it. If it was too dry to farm, they ran water on it so that their crops could grow.

Land that was swampy or marshy was crisscrossed with ditches, and the water slowly drained off. Then the land might be plowed and used for crops. Where red-winged blackbirds, herons and egrets lived before, the farm fields supported field sparrows and meadowlarks. One kind of wildlife was replaced by another.

Westward, on the plains and in the mountain valleys, the land was too dry for farming. From nearby lakes and streams the settlers dug ditches to bring water onto the land. Once irrigated, the land began to produce alfalfa and sugar beets, potatoes and many other crops. Here the familiar songbirds and quail of farmlands took the place of badgers and coyotes.

As irrigated areas spread up the valleys throughout the arid country, there came to be a curious mixing of farm wildlife with other types that lived on the surrounding dry lands. Ground squirrels and pocket gophers took to feeding on the farmer's crops. Jackrabbits and sage grouse developed a liking for alfalfa. In the arid rangeland that stretches between the irrigated areas, badgers and coyotes still live. There in the Far West, as everywhere else, the landscape changed as we settled it and learned to use it. And the wildlife changed with the landscape.

Dry lands have been irrigated

Settlement and wildlife

It took about 300 years to explore and settle the vast area that is now the United States of America. The changes made were enormous. Completely new conditions often replaced the original forests and grasslands. The effect on original wildlife was profound. During that time many kinds of wildlife were almost destroyed by hunting, trapping and, more recently, by poisoning.

Until almost the end of the last century, the biggest problem was to settle the new lands. At first wildlife was valued only as it provided fur, food and, later, plumes for ladies' hats. The big animals, the furbearing animals, the predators, the edible birds, went first. Their numbers were cut down by millions or, in some cases, by billions.

Enormous areas of land were opened up as the forested country was settled. Quail increased. As the second-growth forests came up, deer grew more numerous. Birds and mammals that feed on corn or other grains increased. As people adjusted to the new lands, so wildlife had to adjust.

At the beginning of the present century, we began to realize that we could only have wildlife if we took some action. If we wanted wildlife—for whatever reason—there were two things we would have to do. We would have to provide places where the species could survive and flourish. And we would have to provide them with sufficient protection in that environment.

Bobwhite quail increased with settlement

EXTERMINATION AND SANCTUARY

The extinction of species

Our realization of wildlife needs came a little late for some kinds of animals. By the turn of the century twenty-six kinds of wildlife had become extinct in this country. Since 1900 another twenty-two have disappeared.

There are three reasons why these animals became extinct. The biggest reason of all is probably that they were overkilled by hunters. The second reason is that their habitat was destroyed. The third reason is that we introduced diseases or rats or some other animals that destroyed them or their habitats. We do not know exactly what happened to some of these unfortunate creatures. Anyway, forty-eight species are gone, and human beings are responsible for their going.

The list includes the plains wolf, the sea mink, the eastern and Merriam's elks, the eastern cougar, the badlands bighorn, the Steller's sea cow of the north Pacific and two voles, or mice.

The birds include the Labrador duck, great auk, heath hen, passenger pigeon, three kinds of parakeet, and twenty-six birds of Hawaii. These Hawaiian birds are strange to most of us. They include three thrushes, two rails (a type of shorebird), a honey eater, and a group of others known only by their Hawaiian or Latin names.

Besides these, there are six kinds of fish. These include the San Gorgonio trout, a sucker, and four little fish similar to the devil pupfish described on page 48. Two of these little fish were found to be missing possibly no more than seven years ago.

We very nearly exterminated the American bison

The great auk

Many years ago there used to be a stately bird that ranged along our Atlantic shores, possibly as far south as Florida. It was often called a penguin, but it was not, although it resembled those Antarctic birds. This was the great auk.

These birds were good-natured and therefore easily caught and easily killed. Like penguins, they could not fly. Sailors and fishermen slaughtered them for their flesh or feathers, sometimes by the hundreds. By about 1840, they had disappeared in North America.

On the 6th of June, 1844, the last of the great auks was killed. Three sailors landed on a tiny island off the coast of Iceland. They saw two auks among the numberless seabirds and started after them. The auks ran along a ledge under a cliff, but they were soon caught. The sailors carried them hurriedly down to their boats, for the wind was rising. In a few moments the birds' necks were wrung and the bodies tossed into the boat.

Aside from being edible and producing feathers useful for stuffing pillows, the great auk seems to have been of no particular value to mankind—as far as we know. Anyway, there is no place where the great auk lived that is now exactly the same as it was before the bird was wiped out of existence. We have really no idea what part it played in the natural scheme of things, but if it had not been exterminated, we could still enjoy watching it along our Atlantic shores.

A museum specimen of the great auk

The passenger pigeon

This is a picture of the last passenger pigeon that ever lived. It died in its cage in a Cinncinnati zoo in 1914. These birds were once so abundant that people believed no amount of killing could affect them. But killing did destroy them, and the beautiful soft-winged creatures that once darkened the sky by their very numbers are gone forever.

Alexander Wilson, a famous American ornithologist who died in 1813, once tried to estimate the number of passenger pigeons in a single flock. He watched the flock pass overhead for *four hours.* He said he thought the column was more than a mile wide. It was moving at the rate of about 60 miles an hour. Thus, it was about 240 miles long. If there were three birds per square yard in the mass, then some 2,230 million birds were in this immense flock. Wilson thought this number was probably far below the actual figure.

Stories like this are difficult to believe, even as recounted by scientists. Yet, in 1869, from a single town in Michigan, three carloads of dead pigeons were shipped to market *each day* for forty days. This totalled almost 12 million birds. From another town, 16 million went to market within twenty-four months.

Huge numbers of birds were slaughtered wholesale, wherever the immense flocks flew, until finally there was just one bird left. And then there were none.

The last passenger pigeon

Bison and antelope

As we have already seen, our American bison or buffalo may have numbered 60 million head in primitive times.

The long story of the destruction of the gigantic buffalo herds has been the subject of many books. They don't make particularly pleasant reading. The animals were slaughtered wastefully and wantonly. Finally, by 1903 there were less than a hundred animals in the wild state left in this country. These were in Yellowstone Park and in the Wichita Mountains of Oklahoma. Besides these some other animals were to be found in zoos or game preserves, and some were protected on western ranches, more or less in captivity.

Then the tiny herd in Yellowstone was given real and careful protection. Animals from private collections were added to the herd. The buffalo began to respond and increase. Today we have more than five thousand in our refuges and parks.

Pronghorn antelopes, estimated at some 40 million in the beginning, dropped to about seventeen thousand by 1908. Antelope as well as buffalo were protected in Yellowstone Park. Ranchers protected antelope in various parts of the Plains. If private citizens had not accorded buffalo and antelope the protection they did, neither animal might still be in existence.

With rigid bans on hunting, both animals increased. Animals were livetrapped and transplanted to various refuges to start new herds.

Buffaloes preserved on wild land in Montana

The rare and endangered

The list of birds and mammals that are in danger of becoming extinct in the United States contains seventy-eight names. For most of them the outlook is grim. Some may be saved, but others will probably join the forty-eight already gone. Several have not been seen for many years, and some experts believe they are already extinct.

Each year the Secretary of the Interior is required by law to publish a list of endangered species. The list is put together by scientists, state governments, interested organizations, and the U.S. Fish and Wildlife Service. The list now carries fourteen mammals, thirty-six birds, twenty-two fishes, and six reptiles or amphibians. You can get this list by writing the Secretary of Interior in Washington, D.C.

The grizzly bear is on this list and also the timber wolf, the Florida panther, the black-footed ferret, two types of seals, and two kinds of deer. It also includes the alligator, along with three kinds of cutthroat trout and a number of smaller fish. Whooping cranes, the California condor, three types of geese, the Everglades kite, and the southern bald eagle are on the list. Then there are the ivory-billed woodpecker, masked bobwhite, Attwater's prairie chicken, two sparrows, two warblers and a number of Hawaiian birds.

Some, such as the Eskimo curlew, Bachman's warbler and the Caribbean monk seal, may already have disappeared. The ivory-billed woodpecker, thought to be extinct but apparently sighted in 1967, may be gone very soon. Biologists say we cannot save an animal once its numbers have gone below a certain limit.

The black-footed ferret,
one of the rarest American mammals

Sanctuary

It is a shocking thing to realize that we may have wiped a living creature out of existence. Not one, but a number of species are gone, and it appears likely that more may also become extinct. Human beings are responsible, in one way or another.

In America, during the latter part of the nineteenth century, even as the extermination was taking place, many people began to protest and to try to stop the trend. As you might guess, these people were laughed at. They were considered either eccentric or mentally unbalanced, and they were called "do-gooders," "bird-watchers,"—and a lot worse.

But we have to thank these people for the really remarkable wildlife population in this country. This book is far too small to name the clubs and societies and other organizations involved. There were a great many, and among the leaders was the National Audubon Society. This society is possibly the best known. Certainly it is typical of dedicated wildlife conservation groups.

By about the beginning of this century, public opinion began really to change. Almost all our national wildlife refuges, national forests, national parks, wilderness areas, state refuges, parks, and forests have been set up since 1900. Today we have many millions of acres of land and water either set aside for wildlife or on which wildlife is well protected.

Cormorants find sanctuary on protected, rocky seacoasts

What is a refuge?

Many years ago when a number of kinds of wildlife were rapidly disappearing, a refuge was a place where wildlife was protected. And this meant that wildlife was protected from people. On our first parks and refuges, no hunting whatever was permitted. Such areas were often called inviolate sanctuaries. Inside them wildlife was safe, except from its natural enemies.

But we have learned that this idea is not as sound as we thought. In the areas set aside as refuges, some of the birds or mammals increased in numbers. Pretty soon the refuge could simply not support them. Deer herds ate themselves out of house and home. So did elk herds. The animals began to ruin the trees, gnawing the bark in their efforts to get food.

In our waterfowl refuges the ducks, geese and other water birds sometimes flocked in such numbers that thousands would be weakened or die for lack of enough food. In some of the big game areas, the grazing animals like buffalo could not get enough grass. The ranges became heavily overgrazed. Bears increased until they were first a nuisance, then a real danger to the public. How was this problem solved?

In our national wildlife refuges we now permit carefully regulated hunting to keep the numbers down. We try to keep the population of wildlife up to the maximum numbers the refuge can support. Thus, an area which is a sanctuary this year may be opened to restricted hunting next year—and vice versa.

Safe places for wildlife

National wildlife refuges

Our first official federal wildlife refuge was a little sandy island off the east coast of Florida. There was a nesting colony of brown pelicans on this four-acre area. For some years the state of Florida had been trying to protect the birds from plume-hunters. A scientific society, the American Ornithologists' Union, was cooperating, and indeed had supplied a warden. In 1903 President Theodore Roosevelt signed an order making the island a refuge. The government then took it over, warden and all.

Today we have 321 refuges, with 28.6 million acres inside their boundaries. Two hundred and fifty of these are refuges for migratory waterfowl. Some 40 more are for other migratory birds, and colonies of nesting birds—such as the pelicans on Pelican Island. There are 20 more set aside for endangered species of wildlife. The rest are generally good wildlife environments that accommodate many species.

The very largest of the refuges are places where there is big game, such as buffalo, antelope, elk, grizzly and polar bears, caribou, mountain sheep, moose and the like.

Our biggest refuge is the Arctic National Wildlife Range on the Arctic Ocean in the northeastern corner of Alaska. It contains 8.9 million acres. The largest of all refuges is in Canada. This is the Queen Maud Gulf Migratory Bird Sanctuary with more than 15 million acres. In it waterfowl nest and breed, then migrate south into our country and beyond.

Pelicans in a refuge in California

Refuges in national parks

Our national parks and monuments are also wildlife refuges. They are true sanctuaries in the sense that no hunting is permitted in them.

We have 32 national parks containing 13.6 million acres. And we have 77 national monuments with 8.9 million acres. This makes a total of 22.5 million acres of wildlife refuges.

A national park was really our first federal wildlife refuge, although we did not call it that. This was Yellowstone National Park, an area of better than 2,200,000 acres. The park was established in 1872. All hunting was prohibited in 1894 and has been ever since.

Yellowstone was one of the places where the wild animals increased to numbers greater than the area could support. The elk did this. The bears finally became a nuisance and a few became dangerously troublesome. This was a very serious problem and something had to be done about it.

The solution has been to capture or livetrap enough animals to bring their numbers down to what the park can support. The surplus animals are sent to zoos or to other parks or refuges. Also, special arrangements may be made to hunt the animals that spill over outside the park boundaries. Occasionally a bear that is really dangerous may have to be shot. In this way we try to maintain a balance between wildlife and their habitat.

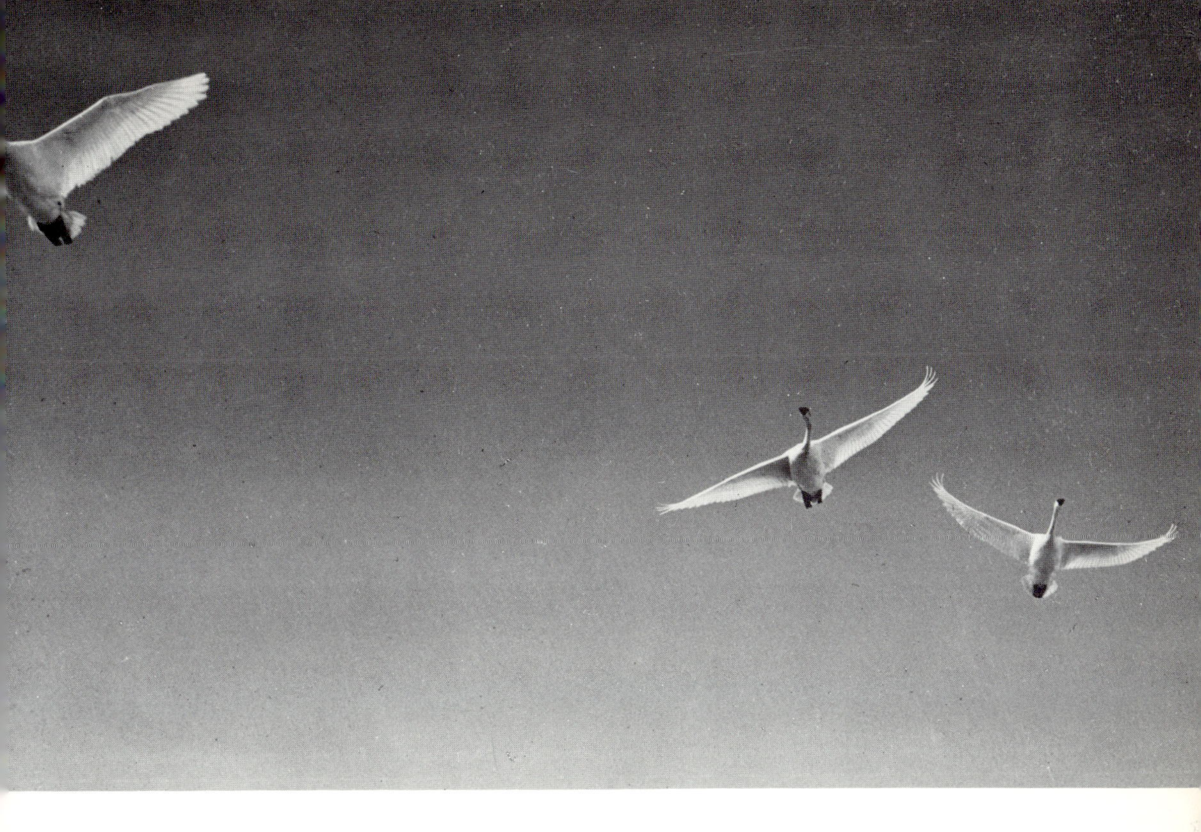

Trumpeter swans find one refuge in a national park

State wildlife refuges

Various states were working at setting up wildlife refuges before the federal government became interested. For example, the state of California created a small waterfowl refuge in 1870, in Oakland. And, as we have already seen, the state of Florida was trying to protect the pelicans on Pelican Island in the 1890s. There were others.

Today the states operate more than 1,700 areas for wildlife. These include 48.5 million acres of land and water.

About 82 percent of these managed areas are useful for upland game, such as quail or pheasants. About 42 percent are valuable for waterfowl, and about 57 percent benefit big game animals. You can see from these figures that the uses of the areas overlap, and that some are valuable for a variety of wild species.

Most of the state refuges are open to hunting and, in fact, hunting of one sort or another is permitted on 47.8 out of 48.4 million acres. Most states control this hunting very carefully. Parts of many refuges may be entirely closed to all hunting. Depending on conditions the hunting season may be restricted or stopped altogether in certain seasons.

Thus, in addition to providing public hunting on a controlled basis, the state refuges are of real value to wildlife. They complement our federal refuges. And they help significantly in keeping up certain of our wildlife populations.

The California condor.
Refuges may not save this largest American bird

Refuges for fish

You can fish in most national parks and monuments and in federal and state refuges. Many of the streams and lakes are restocked frequently with fish that are not native. Perhaps we have not done as much with fish as we have with other forms of wildlife. Even so, there have been some achievements.

In the Amargosa Desert of southern Nevada there are some rare little fishes that live in isolated warm springs. They are found nowhere else in the world. All of them are what fish experts—ichthyologists—call Cyprodonts. This is a family of small fishes most common in tropics.

One of these Cyprodonts is found in a deep pool of warm (92°F.), alkaline water known as Devil's Hole. The spring has been included in Death Valley National Monument to protect a tiny fish known as the devil pupfish. There is a small population of this species living in the upper levels of the pool. The fish are dark brown on the back, with sides of iridescent blue, green or gold. It is believed that they may have been in this spring for several thousand years.

We protect fish in several other places. For example, in a few places in California and western Nevada, the Lahontan cutthroat trout is protected. This is a trout able to withstand the alkali conditions of desert waters. And in Rocky Mountain National Park a few of the streams are off limits to anglers. This is to protect the native greenback trout.

Salmon jumping the falls in Alaska

Summary of refuges

We do not have an inventory of all the land in this country on which wildlife is given protection though we know that the big areas add up to about 107 million acres. These are our national parks and monuments, state parks, and national and state wildlife refuges.

Besides these areas there are many others. They are set up on some of our national forests and on lands administered by other federal and state agencies. Museums, colleges, universities, the Nature Conservancy and the Audubon Society have natural areas on which wildlife is accorded protection. Many thousands of county and municipal parks and forests also serve as wildlife refuges.

Largest of all, perhaps, in area are the hundreds of thousands of wildlife areas on farms and ranches across the country. No one has ever taken an inventory of these. The total land area involved must be several hundreds of million acres.

We should note that on *all* the land and waters of our country, wildlife is protected by our laws that control hunting and fishing.

Americans today are interested and concerned in the conservation of wildlife. We are spending enormous amounts of money to make sure that we keep wild creatures in our country. We are trying to save the rare and vanishing species, from the tiny devil's pupfish to the giant grizzly bear. From these creatures of the wild we may gain information we may one day need about this world in which we live.

Whooping cranes on a national wildlife refuge in Texas

WILDLIFE VALUES AND INTEREST

Interest and beauty

Wildlife is a part of our natural heritage in America. Like our soil, waters, forests, and vast rangelands of the West, wildlife is a valuable resource. Among its many values are its interest and beauty.

Our national emblem is a native bird—the bald eagle. The eagle is on the great seal of the United States, and it has been on our dollar and other coins. You see it on public buildings, on the top of flagpoles and on military insignia. The American bison is on one of our nickels. Its likeness is on many bridges and buildings, and on some of our postage stamps.

Many of our counties, towns, rivers and lakes are named for American wildlife. Buffalo in New York, the Big Horn Mountains of Wyoming, Eagle Valley in Oregon, the Snake River and many other places are named after animals, throughout America.

The early explorers followed buffalo trails over the mountains and across the rivers because the buffalo picked the easiest routes. The Indians also followed these trails, and today our railroads and highways follow them.

In such ways wildlife has influenced the development of America. Besides this, many wild creatures are beautiful animals and they are used in painting and as subjects for poetry. It is a great pleasure to see a deer in the woods, or a wild bear, or watch a pelican dive for fish. Near at home many of us delight in the flashing brilliance of the scarlet tanager, or the bright colors of the bluebird. Sights like these may be remembered and treasured as long as we live.

An artist's painting of snow geese

Strangers

Most of the wildlife you read about in this book is native to America. Some, however, has come from foreign countries, just as the early settlers did. We need to do much more research before we can really decide on the wisdom of foreign introductions.

Many kinds of birds have been introduced, and the great majority of them have failed to survive. However, pigeons, English sparrows and starlings now live with us in our cities. And game birds, such as Hungarian partridge, chukar partridge and ring-necked pheasants are common in some parts of our country.

Among the mammals, house mice and rats follow us wherever we go. In Louisiana marshes a muskratlike animal originally from South America, the nutria, has become well established. We have the mongoose in Puerto Rico and Hawaii. And the European boar is wild in the southern Appalachians, Texas, New Hampshire, California and Hawaii.

There is a great divergence of opinion about bringing in animals from foreign countries. Various states have different laws about this. For example, California law prohibits it; Texas and New Mexico encourage it. In Texas a number of big game animals are now established in the wild. These include the axis, sambar, sika, and fallow deer, barbary sheep, mouflon sheep, aoudad sheep and black-buck antelope. On a Florida island even eland and zebra appear to be successful.

Among game birds, the white-winged pheasant of Afghanistan, Iranian and Korean pheasants, red jungle fowl and both black and gray francolins seem to be increasing in a number of places.

The starling is a bird brought from Europe

Fur

Many of the furbearing animals caught by the early trappers are now very rare. But wild furs are still an important crop. Each year trappers get some 9 million pelts, valued at about 18 million dollars.

Today many of our wild furbearers live where we use the land for growing cultivated crops, pasture or woodland. In thickets and fencerows, along streams and ditches, in farm woodlands and marshes, the furbearers thrive when we give them a chance. The most valuable of them are mink, muskrat, raccoon, skunk and opossum. Other useful but usually less valuable ones are fox, weasel, badger, coyote, squirrel and rabbit.

One of the best of our wild furs is muskrat. Muskrats are common both in salt water marshes along the Atlantic and Gulf coasts, and in freshwater marshes scattered throughout the states. Millions of muskrat pelts are trapped every year from our marshlands. The most valuable crop that can be raised on many of these wet lands is a wildlife crop—muskrats and waterfowl.

Muskrat, raccoon, mink, opossum and skunk are used for making attractive, warm coats. Fur is used extensively to trim coats and other garments. Some kinds of felt are made from fur, especially rabbit. There are also many special uses for our wild furs.

We get many furs from foreign countries, and we raise many furbearers like mink and fox on fur farms. Much of the fur we produce in the United States, however, will continue to come from the wild, as it has in the past.

Marshlands produce good crops of valuable muskrats

Hunting

The American pioneers had to hunt to get meat to eat and skins for making warm clothing. Most of the hunting today, however, is for sport. Each year about 14 million Americans go hunting. They spend more than a billion dollars in doing this.

There is a wonderful variety of hunting in our country. For those who like to hunt in the open, there are quail, pheasant, partridge and cottontail. The farm woods provide ideal squirrel shooting. Those who like the forests can bag ruffed grouse, wild turkey, woodcock, or snipe. For those who prefer big game, there are deer, elk, antelope, bear, and in distant places even moose, mountain goats and mountain sheep. Every year nearly 2 million people hunt waterfowl.

Most of us today live in cities, with their noise, speed and dirt. When a man walks through a quiet field along the border of a woodland looking for quail, the noise and bustle of the city are no longer in his mind. Camping in the deep woods gives the deer hunter a chance to breathe fresh air and get away from a stuffy office and smoke of the city. And when the fisherman wades through the shaded waters of a trout stream, he finds comfort and rest.

Hunting and fishing are traditional in America. The recreational value of wildlife has become more and more important as our cities have grown larger and the machines that surround us have become more complicated and numerous. This is one of the reasons we should work to preserve our wildlife even more now than ever before.

Hunting is one of America's most popular sports

Fishing

There are about 28 million people who go fishing each year in the United States. They spend a total of about 3 billion dollars on this sport.

The variety and extent of sport fishing in America is very great. In quiet ponds there are bluegills, crappie and largemouth bass. From our lakes we catch perch, pike and muskellunge. In some rivers there are still smallmouth bass and other species. In the mountains there are trout of many kinds. Off our coasts tuna, swordfish, sailfish, and other deepwater species provide exciting sport.

Twice as many people fish for sport than hunt. Our nation believes hunting and fishing are the right of every citizen. To hunt or fish in the United States you must buy a license from your state. To hunt waterfowl you must also buy a special federal duck stamp. With a license you can hunt or fish on special public lands and waters and in national forests. You can fish but not hunt in national parks.

Because so many of us want to hunt and fish, we must often ask permission to go on land that is privately owned. A license to hunt or fish does not permit us to trespass on private property, although our laws say that fish and game belong to the state, not to those who own the land. Many landowners do not like sportsmen on their property because they have been known to kill cows and other livestock, to leave gates open, damage fences or start fires. A serious problem of wildlife management is how to settle this matter of hunting and fishing on private lands.

Fishing is popular in streams, ponds, and on the oceans

Business

Wildlife contributes to American business in a wide variety of ways. We have no accurate estimate of the total dollar value of this business, but it must amount to many tens of billions each year.

As we have seen, more than 40 million people hunt or fish. To do this they must have guns and ammunition or rods and tackle. Many of them camp out and require tents, sleeping bags and other kinds of gear. These sportsmen travel some 30 billion passenger-miles in a year, mostly in automobiles.

We also have more than 8 million people who are interested in observing and studying wildlife, plus another 3 million who are wildlife photographers. They need cameras, binoculars and other equipment to pursue their hobby. They, too, travel a great deal.

Wildlife and sporting books and magazines make business for printers, publishers, authors, booksellers and others.

There are scientific and popular publications on birds, mammals, fish, snakes, insects and other forms of wildlife.

Many landowners now make money from permitting hunting or fishing on their property. Sometimes farmers or ranchers form a group to sell hunting permits on a large area of land. Sportsmen also form hunting or fishing clubs that rent or buy land or water areas to use for sport. All such activities make business.

Wildlife supports a big business

Friends for the farmer

The red-tailed hawk on the opposite page has just caught a mouse. It will eat it or feed it to its young. Rats, mice, and other small rodents as well as insects are favorite foods of owls and hawks. Rodents eat stored seed, girdle trees and carry disease. Harmful insects cause great destruction of cultivated crops, orchards, forest trees and ornamental plants.

Many young birds eat more than their own weight of food each day. Scientists have found 250 tent caterpillars in the stomach of a yellow-billed cuckoo. They found a flicker that had eaten 5,000 ants, and a nighthawk with a stomachful of 500 mosquitoes.

Birds also eat a great many weed seeds, although so many weed seeds are produced that birds may not help to control them as much as they do insects. A bobwhite quail ate 1,700 weed seeds at one meal. The stomach of a snowbird was found that contained 1,500 pigweed seeds. A mourning dove had eaten 7,500 seeds of wood sorrel.

Mammals also help the farmer. Bats eat quantities of mosquitoes. Woodchucks like to eat June beetles. Although the mole disturbs our lawns and eats earthworms, more than half its diet consists of harmful insects such as cutworms and rosebug larvae. The skunk feeds mostly on insects such as grasshoppers, beetles and tobacco worms. The armadillo lives almost entirely on insects, many of them harmful kinds.

The wise farmer knows that most of the time wildlife is helping him. He knows that it is better to work with nature than to work against it.

A red-tailed hawk catches a mouse

Bird migration

Many of our wildlife refuges are for migrating birds. They provide places for the birds to rest or feed or breed. There are some interesting questions about migration. Most people know that birds fly south in the fall, north in the spring. But why do birds do this? How do they know which direction to fly? How do they keep on course in bad weather? How do they know when to start?

Biologists have worked on these problems for many years. They have used radar, airplanes, laboratory studies and birdbanding in their research. And they have learned that the problems are much more complex than they thought.

Birdbanding is a method of study that has provided some of the answers. By now, roughly 15 million birds have had tiny metal or plastic bands attached to one of their legs. The bands carry a number. Most of them read "Notify Fish and Wildlife Service, Washington, D. C." Knowing where and when a bird was banded and where it was found later tells us something about its travels.

The biologists who study birds—ornithologists—have plotted the main migration routes of many birds. We now know pretty well where the birds fly.

We have learned a great deal from these birdbanding studies. Some of the things we have learned are dramatic and surprising. Some we simply cannot explain.

These wild Canada geese wear bird bands

Bird flights

Beside the general flyways of migrating birds, we have learned other things. Some birds fly only short distances. Others fly thousands of miles north and south each year. Not all the flying is in a straight line; the birds may change direction at certain points.

The American golden plover nests in arctic Canada. As fall approaches, it flies southeast to Nova Scotia and Newfoundland. Then it turns due south and flies 2,000 miles over the Atlantic Ocean. It keeps on going, across the Amazon to northern Argentina in South America. When spring comes, the plover flies northwest across South America. It flies clear to Mexico, still going northwest. Then it turns north. It flies across our Great Plains and north to the arctic Canada area again. The young plovers take the route through Mexico in the fall as well as in the spring.

Some birds migrate during the daytime, stopping to rest and feed only at night. Others travel entirely at night. Some fly just above the ocean waves. Others, such as geese, have been seen flying at more than 29,000 feet. Mallards, hummingbirds and some others fly at about 60 miles an hour. Most small songbirds fly at 30 miles per hour.

The little hummingbirds fly 500 miles across the Gulf of Mexico in a single night. The longest flights of all are made by the graceful arctic tern. This bird travels about 9,500 miles from the Arctic to the Antarctic.

Many birds, including these Canada geese, make their migratory flights at night

Why birds migrate

Ornithologists now believe that birds start to migrate because of internal changes in their bodies. The birds become ready to breed at regular periods, closely related to their times of migration. They fly north in order to breed where conditions are better for raising young birds.

Northward the days are longer. There is more time to feed the young nestlings, and hence the nestlings grow faster. This is a critical time, for many prowling animals feed on young birds. The quicker the nestlings can be got ready to fly, the better.

The biologists have also found out that migratory birds are clearly able to tell directions from the sun. Birds flying at night determine their directions from the moon and from the stars. This is astonishing. It is as though the birds have a built-in sun-compass or star-compass. With this they can navigate.

Even if you have a compass, however, you need a map as well to know where you're going. How do birds manage? The birds know which direction is which. But how does a bird know to fly south or north? And how far? And when to turn? Or how to make up for getting blown off course by strong winds?

There are many questions still to be answered. But we do know that our system of refuges is important and helpful to these migrating birds. Strung out along the flyways, the refuges enable the birds to rest and feed when they must.

Helpless nestlings grow faster, leave the nest sooner in the North

Wildlife and the law

The first American game law was passed one hundred years before the Declaration of Independence, when Connecticut made it unlawful to kill game at certain seasons of the year. Before we became a nation, deer, ruffed grouse, quail, wild turkey and heath hens were protected by various states.

We now have hundreds of laws about wildlife. Some prohibit hunting when wildlife is nesting or caring for its young. Others limit the numbers of quail or rabbits or other kinds of wildlife that you may shoot in a single day or season. Laws tell when you may fish, how many fish you may catch and how big they must be. Automatic shotguns and gun silencers are generally outlawed. Laws regulate payment for damages by wildlife, as when deer eat farm crops.

Not all wildlife laws relate to game animals hunted for sport. It is illegal to sell feathers, quills, plumes and other parts of wild birds. At one time the magnificent snowy egret shown in the picture was nearly exterminated because people killed it to get its beautiful delicate plumes for trimming women's hats. This splendid bird is plentiful now because laws were passed to protect it.

Ever since Massachusetts in 1818 passed the first law to protect a nongame bird, the robin, we have given more and more protection to wildlife. We protect all songbirds, for example. Probably no other country in the world defends its wildlife as well as we do.

The snowy egret is now protected by law from plume hunters

Public support

Laws must be enforced if they are to do what we want them to do. Today almost all states have special uniformed, well-instructed game wardens who help people live up to the wildlife laws of the state. The warden in the picture is enforcing a wildlife law. He is checking to see if the hunters have licenses. Because waterfowl like ducks and geese migrate across so many states and are controlled by federal law, they are protected by federal wardens.

There are a number of government organizations that help to support wildlife. The U. S. Fish and Wildlife Service looks after the management of national wildlife refuges, aids farmers and ranchers with the control of harmful wildlife, deals with commercial fisheries problems and in other ways helps with national wildlife activities. Some other federal agencies give special attention to wildlife in their regular work, especially the Forest Service, Park Service and Soil Conservation Service.

The states, as well as the national government, consider wildlife to be an important natural resource and spend money to study and manage it. In each state there is a Conservation or Fish and Game Department that studies the wildlife of the state, manages state lands set aside for refuges and hunting areas, enforces wildlife laws and carries on other wildlife work. Many states maintain large staffs of well-trained people to conduct this kind of work.

A game warden talks over laws and regulations with hunters

WILDLIFE NEEDS AND PROBLEMS

Wildlife needs—cover

A brushy fencerow, a grapevine tangle, a tuft of grass or a pile of rocks—all these and others like them are cover for wild creatures of some sort. Within these places of refuge wildlife can rest, feed, sleep and raise young in safety. Each type of wildlife must have cover of the right kind, or it cannot survive.

Every wild species has its enemies. The first thing most wild animals do at a sign of danger is to dash for the nearest place of safety. Cover that protects an animal this way is called escape cover by the biologists.

Nesting cover is very important for birds. In its shelter a young brood can be cared for until the little birds can shift for themselves. It may be used only during the breeding season, but it is completely necessary then.

Winter cover is also very important, especially where snow lingers on the ground. In cold country, the evergreen pines and spruces are very valuable to wildlife. They provide a place where some animals can survive during severe cold spells. If winter cover is not available, many birds and mammals freeze to death.

There is a hawthorn in the picture that offers nesting and escape cover. Wild creatures could scarcely hide in it when the leaves have fallen off. Still, its thorny branches might save a bird from a pursuing hawk. Nests of three seasons in the hawthorn show how mockingbirds have used it each spring.

A game warden talks over laws and regulations with hunters

Hawthorn makes good cover for nests

Wildlife needs—food

Everyone knows that all living things must have food to keep alive. We also know that most creatures are not able to obtain food unless it is reasonably close to cover.

For a good many years scientists have been studying the diet of wild creatures. We are still learning many interesting and useful things about wildlife foods. We know, for example, that most of our common birds and animals are of value to agriculture because they eat insect pests or weed seeds.

Frequently the food of young animals is different from the food they eat when they are older. Many young birds in the nest are fed insects by their parents. Later, when they forage for themselves, they may change to a diet of seeds and berries and live almost entirely on plant foods.

Many animals eat different things at different seasons. Bobwhite quail might do very well in spring, summer and fall when different kinds of foods are always present on the ground. When heavy snows come, however, there must be some plants with seeds above the snow, if the bobwhite is to live through the winter.

Some wild creatures eat both plant and animal foods. The menu of the raccoon regularly includes crayfish and wild fruits. Many other animals live almost entirely on other kinds of wildlife. Weasels, hawks and owls are carnivores of this sort. Owls, for example, catch and eat many small rodents like mice.

All wild things spend a great deal of time looking for food. And always they must be alert for creatures larger than themselves that are also looking for a meal.

The food of a young screech owl includes insects

Wildlife needs—water

Just as all wild creatures must have food, so they must have water to drink. This is just as important for them as it is for us. But they do not all get water from a lake or stream or spring. Some kinds of wildlife do very well on the juices of fruits or berries. Some use dew, or get water from insects they eat.

Raspberries and blackberries are popular among the juicy fruits. Mulberries, too, offer a drink to many creatures, including hundreds of kinds of birds.

A pond attracts great numbers of birds and mammals. Surprisingly small bodies of water may be of key importance to wildlife in dry places. Even a tank or trough of water set out for livestock to drink attracts many kinds of wild animals. In some parts of the Southwest, ranchers who want quail put out watering stations just for these birds. The little tanks make it possible for a whole covey of quail to live in a place where they otherwise would never be found.

All the water-loving animals must have free, open water, of course. The water is useful to them for more than drinking and bathing. It may serve to protect them. Canada geese often build their nests on old stumps sticking out of the water or on little islands. Beavers build their houses out in the water. So do muskrats. In this way many water animals protect themselves from their enemies.

Antelope find water to drink at a spring

Interspersion

For wild creatures to make the best use of them, food and cover must be well mixed. This mixing is called *interspersion*. Biologists will tell you that if the interspersion is first rate, wildlife will usually be abundant.

A great open field of wheat or corn is by no means as attractive to wildlife as a grain field well broken up with hedges or brushy fencerows. A deep forest is not particularly good either, except for squirrels and tree-living birds. But if the woods have occasional open glades, they become useful to a good many kinds of birds and mammals, including deer.

Wherever a strip of good cover runs through an open area, it makes a travel lane for wildlife. An excellent example is a hedge running through a farm field. In the protection of these narrow lanes of cover, wild animals can move safely from one place to another.

Streambanks well covered with trees and shrubs make meandering travel lanes through farm country. As the streams branch and wander through fields and woods, they make highways for wildlife through the whole area. The interspersion is good.

The better the interspersion, the better the habitats for pest-destroying birds and mammals that benefit the farmer. Where the interspersion is first rate there will be more wild creatures, and they will cover more territory. Thus it is that farmers as well as wildlife benefit from the scattered distribution of patches of cover.

This land has well scattered cover and travel lanes for wildlife

Enemies of wildlife

All wild species have enemies that prey upon them. It is just as important for wild creatures to protect themselves as it is for them to have food, cover and water.

Sometimes, in order to get food, wild animals prey upon our domestic flocks. Coyotes may kill lambs. Weasels may kill chickens. Some hawks may also kill poultry. In fish hatcheries, herons and kingfishers may catch young fish. Wherever we raise fish, poultry or livestock, we may have to protect them against their enemies. If there is plenty of food for these predators, they will bother our domestic animals less.

Sportsmen often want to kill animals that attack the kinds of wildlife they want to hunt. They want to get rid of skunks because skunks sometimes eat pheasant's eggs. They want to kill hawks because hawks catch quail. But eggs and small birds are among the natural foods of these animals. We cannot change their habits of eating. Furthermore, skunks eat great quantities of harmful insects, and hawks kill a great many mice and rats. Usually when we interfere unwisely with the natural scheme of things, we only make trouble for ourselves.

We can do most to help wildlife guard itself against predators if we provide it with the right kind of home. For example, the bobwhite likes to be near good cover, like a plum thicket or an overgrown fencerow. If we provide cover like this, hawks will not be able to catch so many of them. By making or preserving good wildlife habitat, we can help to protect it against its enemies—and we need not waste time killing predators.

The fox leaves feathers of the ruffed grouse it killed in the snow

Pesticides

Before World War II, we killed insect pests by spraying them with non-persistent chemicals. These were chemicals which broke down and became harmless in a matter of weeks.

But research during the war and after provided us with poisonous sprays that are *persistent.* These chemicals may last a long time, even years. You may know some of them—DDT, lindane, chlordane, and a host of others. We spray our American landscape with upwards of a billion pounds a year of such persistent chemicals now. We do this to kill insect pests, weeds, rats, fungi and other pests we want to get rid of.

We have not been too careful with these sprays. We may kill the insect pest, but in doing so the spray used may also kill useful insects that feed on the insect pest. The spray may kill fish, frogs, crabs and other organisms that live in rivers or lakes. It may kill many kinds of birds as well as mammals.

Many of the side effects are indirect. The chemicals get into creeks and streams as water carries them off the land. Small organisms absorb some. Bigger organisms—minnows, small fish—feed on the small organisms. Fish-eating birds eat the fish—and pick up the chemical. There is a whole series of chain reactions. Worse yet, the chain may finally include human beings who eat the fish or the birds. The effects are not always certainly known.

We are now using such chemicals much more carefully. It pays *always* to be sure of results.

Spraying chemicals may do more damage than we intend

The wildlife environment

Every animal must have the kind of place to live that suits it. That place has to be provided with plenty of the proper food, water and cover. The interspersion—the mix—of food and cover must be good. Hunting and trapping cannot be allowed to become too rigorous. Given these things, wildlife can survive. For each kind of creature, the food, cover and interspersion may need to be different from others. If any one of these items is missing, wildlife will be missing too.

Making wildlife at home on all our land is the only way we can have all the wildlife we want in our country. We already know that refuges plus control of hunting are not enough to provide us with all the wild creatures we need and wish to have. Wildlife needs to be made at home almost everywhere. And almost everywhere in America, the land is used for agriculture—the growing of cultivated crops, grazing of pasture and rangeland and management of forests and woodlots.

The remainder of this book tells about the many kinds of places there are for wildlife in this country. It tells about wildlife and the land on which it must live. And since most land is used for agriculture, the following pages deal mostly with the way wildlife fits into this kind of land use. Eighty-five percent of the United States is used for farming and ranching. This means that making wildlife at home on farms and ranches is one of the most important kinds of wildlife conservation work we can do in America.

Where the land is well used,
wildlife and people prosper

Where the land is well used,
wildlife and people prosper

WILDLIFE ON THE LAND

Wildlife on cropland

There are some areas in our country where there is practically no place for wildlife at all. Great fields of plowed land, kept bare sometimes the year round, are places like this. So are vast areas of wheat or corn or soybeans. Songbirds may fly across them, but they cannot live on them. Quail, pheasants, or other game birds may venture into them a little way if there are crops on the ground, but seldom when they are bare.

Besides being no place for wildlife, bare land is also in danger itself. If it dries out, winds can begin to blow the soil away. This has happened in many states, notably in the infamous Dust Bowl. There are, in fact, a number of little dust bowls in this country where wind erosion is very serious indeed. Some of them are in the East. In such areas agriculture may be in trouble, and wildlife is absent.

There is danger for bare land in the wetter parts of our country too. Rain beating on unprotected soil will wash the soil away, even on quite gentle slopes. There is no place here, either, for wildlife populations.

However, in the last three decades there have been some notable changes on cultivated land. Instead of open cultivated fields of vast extent, our farmers are using strip-cropping. In this method, crops are grown on the contour, thick-growing grasses and legumes alternating with cultivated crops. Strip-cropping protects the soil, provides more variety in vegetation for wildlife, and helps keep silt out of streams. Fish benefit, land animals benefit and the land is kept in good shape.

Strip cropping increases edge of value to wildlife

Wildlife on pasturelands

Pastures vary in different parts of the country. They may be fields of lush grasses, or they may be three or four feet deep with sweetclover, or they may be a mixture of grasses and alfalfa. In any case, they are areas grazed by livestock.

If the grazing is too close so that cover is poor, both the land and wildlife may be in trouble. There is danger to the land because poor pastures are subject to erosion. Since good cover is so important in habitats, wildlife suffers in areas where cover is poor. And, of course, overgrazed pasture doesn't produce much livestock.

Pastures usually require stock-watering ponds. There may be a number of these ponds if the pasture is a large one. They help to keep the livestock well distributed so that local overgrazing does not take place. These ponds are fenced with a water trough outside. If they are properly planned, with some good cover around their shores, these ponds are useful for many kinds of wildlife, especially waterfowl.

Here and there in most pastures are clumps of trees or irregular patches of shrubs on land unsuited to grass. In such areas, wildlife can live and shelter.

If the grazing is well-managed, the grass or legume cover is generally useful to wildlife that inhabits grassy areas. The cover protects the soil, and also produces the maximum forage for livestock.

A fenced pond in a pasture makes a good place for wildlife

Field borders

The edge of a field next to a woods can be a worthless place to a farmer. It does not produce much because the tree roots claim most of the plant food and moisture. The crop plants grow poorly, if at all, in the shade.

If the edge of the field slopes downhill, water runs freely over the bare soil and cuts a small channel. Eventually the channel may get very deep and form a gully. This is especially true in the South.

But we know a way to make these field edges valuable, attractive and safe from erosion. We plant them to special kinds of plants that make a dense cover that stops erosion. Then the borders help to keep the forest from pushing into the field. If the special plants are not too tall, they make a good place to turn the plow or drive wagons around the field. They may even be cut for hay. Some are good honey plants.

In some parts of the country alfalfa and clovers may be used on borders. There are a few grasses that will grow there, too. In the South, field border plants that are successful are perennial and shrubby lespedezas. The lespedezas, like the clovers and other legumes, are good for the soil.

Field borders provide excellent cover and food for wildlife—indeed they are often called wildlife borders. They are especially attractive to birds. There are many thousands of miles of these borders on farms now, and they are making a great difference to quail and other birds that use them for homes and travel lanes.

An excellent wildlife border of shrub lespedeza in South Carolina

Wildlife areas

On almost every farm there are some places that are not worth farming. There are stony spots, wet areas or rough, rugged slopes that are too steep to cultivate. There are also patches of very poor land known best to the farmer who tries to work them. Generally these areas seem to be a nuisance. It is not worth using seed and fertilizer on them. Even so, they are sometimes plowed and planted, just to avoid the trouble of going around them.

Many of these small areas ought to have plants growing on them for the good of the land itself. If they are not so protected, soil may wash off them onto the fields below. Wild plants or "brush" that grows on them should not be cleared off, nor should they be burned. They should also be protected from grazing livestock. Big trees that grow on these spots may have to be cut so that the crops are not shaded, but as a general rule, the areas should be given planned protection.

In these islands of cover, songbirds live, feeding on insect pests in the fields around them. In some of them furbearers like the skunk find a home, and cottontail rabbits are frequently found there. Wildlife islands help interspersion, and they make excellent coverts for quail and other game. Sometimes farmers plant evergreens in such areas for winter cover. Sometimes, too, special shrubs are planted there to supply food as well as cover for valuable farm allies. Such areas are indeed wildlife land, and so they should remain.

A planted and protected head of a gully makes an excellent wildlife area

Hedges

Many kinds of wildlife use hedges, all or part of the year. Insect-eating birds nest in them and feed their young on pests from the crop fields. The more hedges there are, the more help the farmer gets. Game birds use them, and hunters often get their bag from the coveys that live along these travel lanes.

When a hedge is planted across the slope of a hill, it helps to prevent soil from washing down the slope. If the hedge is on the level, or contour, it will curve back and forth as the slope of the hill changes. You can prove this to yourself by walking along the side of a hill on the same level. Your steps will lead you in easy curves *out* on the bulges, and *in* on the hollows.

On the upper side of a hedge, soil may pile up as water carries it down the slope. If the shrubs are thickly planted, little soil gets through. Where farmers cannot use terraces to save their soil, hedges may be just the thing. Hedges also make good fences, if they are made of the right kind of plant.

Hedges are not hard to keep in shape. They need no pruning if they consist of shrubs that will not spread. Beach plum, cranberry bush, shrub lespedeza, multiflora rose, privet and bayberry make good hedges. Good hedges are far more common in Europe and the British Isles than they are in America. People there have learned their values after many centuries of farming. One day we may have as many as they do, and as good ones.

Hedges are good places for fruit-producing

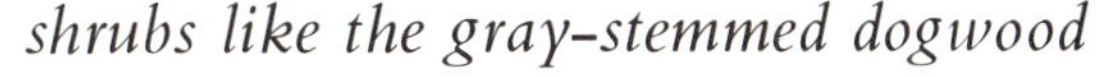

shrubs like the gray-stemmed dogwood

Windbreaks

Strong winds blow in some sections of our country, hard enough to whip dry unprotected soil right off the top of the ground. This sort of thing is common in flat open country where there are few or no trees. Wind erosion is an ever-present danger in many parts of the Great Plains and the far West.

One way to slow down the wind and stop wind erosion is to plant a windbreak of trees and shrubs across the path of the commonest winds. Windbreaks may be made up of several rows of trees with a row or two of shrubs on the outer sides. Or they may be only a single row of trees or shrubs. In either case they act to keep the wind from getting a good sweep across the land.

Windbreaks also protect crops from drying out in the wind. They make life more pleasant in any farmstead when they are planted around buildings. They produce fruits for jams and jellies.

The wildlife value of windbreaks is considerable. They may offer the only cover in regions otherwise treeless. Pheasants regularly use them for headquarters. Many songbirds nest in the protection of the foliage. When windbreak shrubs are selected for the food they produce for wildlife, they are doubly valuable.

Most windbreaks have a row or two of evergreen trees such as pines or spruces. The protection of these evergreens means a great deal to wildlife that spends the winter there. Often these evergreens afford the only cover during the winter season, which is always critical for wildlife.

Windbreaks protect the land and offer cover for game birds like the ringneck pheasant in the lower picture

Ditches

In various parts of the United States there are ditches that have been dug to drain wet lands. In other places there are irrigation ditches to make dry lands wet enough to farm. We have hundreds of thousands of miles of such ditches. Many of them are good for wildlife, especially if there is vegetation on the banks.

Along the grassy margins of big main ditches, you can often find ducks and other waterfowl nesting. Smaller ditches are favorite places for some of the furbearers like mink, raccoon and especially muskrat. In Ohio and Indiana, cornfields that have brush-covered ditches running across them make excellent homes for ring-necked pheasants.

Some farmers dig ditches in their marshes to make travel lanes for muskrats and to get more marsh plants which the muskrats use for food. Sometimes the muskrats make their dens in the ditch banks. After marshes are ditched, they produce several times as many muskrats as before. This is an example of how ditches can be used to make better homes for wildlife.

Soil conservationists know the suitable plants to grow on ditchbanks so the banks will not erode and wash soil into the ditches. Much money can be saved if the ditches do not have to be dredged clean so often. If the kind of plants grown on the banks are selected for their wildlife food and cover values as well as their ability to hold the soil, there is a double advantage.

Ditchbanks protected by shrubs and grass make homes for wildlife

Spoilbanks

On more than 3 million acres in the United States, the surface layers have been torn up and piled aside in order to get at the coal or other minerals underneath. We call this strip mining or surface mining. The soil and lower layers that are piled up we call spoilbanks. At the rate the work is going on, another 2 million acres will be torn up by 1980.

Strip mining defaces the landscape, and of course, destroys wildlife habitats. Streams are also affected. Nearly 13,000 miles of streams are already adversely affected as well as nearly 500 lakes and reservoirs. Every state is involved, although more than half the land involved is in the Appalachian states of the East.

If spoilbanks are protected from fire, a natural vegetation grows over most of them. Within a few years they are covered with weeds and briars. Finally scattered seedlings of elm, sycamore, locust or other trees appear. Then they make good homes for quail, pheasants, rabbits, squirrels and opossums.

Spoilbanks usually have to be fifteen or twenty years old before they are weathered enough to support trees. Then trees good enough for lumber can be grown on them. Some spoilbanks that are not too rough can be used soon after mining for making pasture.

Usually the low spots in strip-mined lands fill up with water and become ponds. The ponds and the land around them make good places for fish, muskrat, mink and raccoon. Strip-mined areas several years old usually produce so much wildlife that they are favorite places to trap, hunt or fish.

Spoilbanks from strip-mining make excellent wildlife habitats when treated, as in the lower picture

Gullies for wildlife

Where land has been farmed the wrong way for a long time, gullies form in it. Water running downhill makes a little waterfall where it drops from a high place to a low place. As the water pours over the edge, it cuts away the soil. The longer the water flows, the more it cuts.

Gullies can become very large. They may cut clear across a whole county and swallow up roads, buildings and much good farm land. Every state has gullies. Some have more than others. But wherever gullies get a good start, it means that the land is being unwisely used.

If the farmer begins to practice soil conservation, which is the best way to farm we know, gullies often become very good places for wildlife. When all the land *above* the gully is farmed correctly, much less water runs into the gully. If a little water still comes occasionally, the farmer digs a ditch that carries the water away from the place where the gully begins.

Next, the conservation farmer puts a fence around the gully to keep livestock out. The fence may be made of roses or some other thorny bush that livestock cannot push through. In the gully the farmer may plant grass, or shrubs and trees.

Plants grown in gullies make good cover and produce food for wildlife. Then the gully makes a good home for quail, pheasants and many other birds as well as fur animals like the skunk, opossum and raccoon.

Eroded land makes a place for wildlife, as in the lower picture

Streambanks

There are about three million miles of streams in the United States. Their banks used to be well clothed with trees, shrubs and grasses. These plants protected the banks against the cutting of the stream itself.

As we cleared the land, the banks of many of our streams were cleaned off and left naked. When the spring floods came, the rushing waters cut away the banks. The more the banks were cut away, the more good bottomland was destroyed. In addition to silt coming downstream from farm fields above, the banks themselves help to fill the stream as they cave in.

But the streambanks can be protected from grazing animals so that trees and shrubs and other plants can start to grow on them. Sometimes the banks have to be sloped and planted. When this is done, the banks are stabilized and the stream stops cutting.

This type of work also makes the land a better place for wildlife. The edge of a protected stream is a favorite place for raccoons. Kingfishers live there. Songbirds of many kinds make their homes in the cover along the banks. Even beavers may come back and settle on the streams.

We have already seen how a stream with good vegetation on each bank provides a fine travel lane for farm wildlife. The plants also help to keep the stream cool, and to make the water a clearer and better place for fish. All told, when a streambank is well covered it is of great value for the land and for wildlife.

Streambanks, when properly protected, as in the lower picture, can be of great value to wildlife

Silted stream

In a flooding stream the water is usually filled with silt that comes from every creek and rivulet along the river's course. This silt comes off the land wherever the soil is not well covered. It clogs our streams, fills our ponds and settles in our reservoirs. Every year in the United States siltation causes damage costing millions.

Many of our best fish cannot live in muddy waters. Their places are taken by less desirable fish like carp, that do not mind silt. In the rivers of the Ohio Valley, the water used to be so clear that many mussels lived there. Their shells were collected to make buttons. As the stream became muddy, the mussels began to disappear and finally the button business also disappeared.

Along the sea coasts, where the rivers pour tons upon tons of eroded soil, the bottoms of the bays become so soft and muddy that oysters can no longer find a place to fasten and grow. With water life as with land life, where the home is destroyed wildlife is gone.

Muddy water shuts out the light, which is needed by tiny water plants. Silt also blankets the bottoms of streams and kills water insects that live there and are used by fish for food. Where silt settles it destroys nesting places for fish that need clean bottom for spawning. It often settles waste materials like sewage and chemicals in the stream, thus decreasing the amount of oxygen. Silt may even clog the gills of fish, and injure the breathing structures of other water life.

Streams filled with silt are very poor places for fish

Pollution

Too many of our streams and rivers, lakes and estuaries are polluted. They are a hazard to health and we cannot use them for swimming, or other water sports. Fish and waterfowl cannot use them either.

We are doing a great deal these days to clean up our streams. Our national Water Resources Council reports that for the first time in history we now have good water quality standards for the vast majority of the nation's waters. This means that most states now have anti-pollution laws that can be enforced and that will be effective.

Many things have to be done to improve the quality of our waters. As we have already noted, a major source of pollution is from erosion sediment. This must be kept from streams by widespread use of soil conservation measures.

We must treat industrial and city wastes before they are released into our streams. A little better than half the population of our cities is now served by satisfactory disposal methods. But the remainder either has none at all, or the treatment is inadequate. This is a problem we must solve if our waters are to be as clean as we wish. We have another problem too in the several million tons of acids that flow into our streams every year from old mines.

To do the total clean up job may take a billion dollars a year for quite a few years ahead. If we undertake this immense task—and we have already made a good start—we may hope to have all our streams, lakes and estuaries clear and clean everywhere. This will mean a better and more beautiful countryside, to say nothing of more places for water sports, including fishing and swimming.

A clear stream is a valuable resource and a thing of beauty

The pond

Of all the places to see wildlife, a pond is one of the best. There ducks and geese feed in the water, or nest in the grassy margin. Along the shore are sandpipers, killdeer, avocets, curlews, herons, cranes and other fascinating birds. Mammals like the raccoon, muskrat and even the mink will be found there. Frogs, snakes, turtles and many lesser forms of life are at every pond, making it one of the most interesting places on the farm.

More and more ponds are being built in the United States. They furnish water for livestock in pastures, for spraying orchards, irrigating gardens and for fire protection. Or they may be used for raising fish. Whatever their special purpose, they make ideal homes for a great variety of wild creatures.

A pond is most valuable to wildlife when it is fenced. This keeps grazing cattle out and creates a small refuge. The millions of ponds that have been constructed by farmers and ranchers throughout the country are especially important to waterfowl for nesting and feeding.

Shrubs and vines like rose, wild plum, bittersweet, dogwood, grape, bayberry and Russian olive are often planted around a pond for the food they provide, and for cover. Pines, spruce and cedar are planted in clumps in the fence corners for shelter during the winter. Many kinds of wildlife that may never have been seen on the farm or ranch before a pond was built, soon afterward make permanent homes there.

Ponds are useful for Canada geese

Ponds for fishing

Perhaps you have read about fertilizing a pond to raise fish. The fertilizer furnishes chemicals which, together with sunlight, carbon dioxide and water are used by tiny water plants to make food. These plants are used for food by microscopic animals. The tiny animals, in turn, are eaten by insects. The insects are eaten by certain kinds of fish, like sunfish. The sunfish are eaten by carnivorous fish like bass. Both sunfish and bass are good food for man. Fertilized water will support about twice as much fish as water that is not fertilized.

Enough fertilizer has been put in the water when it turns a greenish brown color from the tiny plants. This color is called "water bloom." Then young fish are put in the pond—a hundred largemouth black bass and a thousand bluegill sunfish for each acre of water. After a year, fishing can begin. The water is fertilized several times each summer to keep plenty of food chemicals in it. From an acre pond you can catch around two hundred pounds of fish every year. This is as much meat as a good pasture produces.

A good fish pond must have a wide dam to keep the water about eight feet deep, with a spillway to carry the water around the dam during floods. The edges of the pond should be steep so they do not become filled with shallow water plants. The pond should be built on any soil heavy enough to hold water where there is a depression and a suitable amount of land above to collect plenty of rainwater. The land above should all be farmed the conservation way so the silt will be kept out of the pond.

In the pond, tasty fish can be caught for food

Beaver

Because of his dam building, the beaver has been called the first American soil conservationist. He has also been called our first up-stream engineer. Dams built by beavers held back flood waters for a million years before America was settled. Behind the dams, silt gradually filled in, and thus the beaver helped to build flat river valleys from narrow ravines.

High up at the very beginnings of our rivers, we can use many thousands of little dams. We need them to hold back floodwater. We also need them to help build up the beds of the little streams that have been cutting deep since we cleared the land. These dams would cost us millions of dollars in taxes if we had to build them. Instead, we are capturing beavers where they can still be found and releasing them along the creek banks.

In the little tributaries of our rivers, the beavers are working for America once more. Wherever there is aspen or poplar or willow—enough to use for dam building and food—the beavers settle down and build their dams. Because our streams have more silt in them now, the beaver ponds fill up rapidly. Sometimes a dam three or four feet high will fill up in a few weeks. The beavers then build another dam. A dozen beavers and their offspring are known to have built sixty dams in five miles of stream in a period of two years.

The beaver is the nation's foremost wildlife citizen. His useful activities and his remarkable industry make him the animal that has contributed the most to his country.

Upstream engineering by beavers

Rangeland

Range is different from pasture. On pastureland we plant one or two grasses and a legume or two. Rangelands support a wide variety of grasses and other plants. They are native plants that occur in what are called plant communities. Getting these natural plant communities to produce the most possible forage for livestock—or big game—is known as range management.

Most people think of rangeland as being out West. It is true that there are vast areas in the drier western half of our country that are managed for livestock production. This is the great western range. Grasses and shrubs clothe most of it; trees are present only in the higher elevations.

But every state has at least some native range within its borders—even Rhode Island and Delaware. Some of our southern states have more range than Utah or Nevada which form part of our western range.

Range in excellent condition can support maximum numbers of livestock. It is about twice as useful for wildlife as poor range. This is why wildlife conservationists have such an interest in good range management.

Wonderful progress is being made in improving our native range. Productivity of forage and numbers of the livestock feeding on it have increased spectacularly in recent years. Even so, range management specialists think we could still double the productivity if all range were properly treated. This would be a big gain for wildlife too.

The western range supports livestock and big game such as elk

Unwanted wildlife

On western rangelands prairie dogs, kangaroo rats, ground squirrels, gophers and jack rabbits are common. They have been poisoned almost everywhere because people thought they ate grass that the cattle and sheep should have. Biologists have learned, however, that range rodents eat more weeds than they do grass. This is the reason there are more of them on overused rangeland where weeds are abundant than there are where the grass is plentiful. Where the land is not used wisely we may often have trouble with wild animals.

Wolves, like the one in the picture, are rare now in the United States. They were killed because they attacked cattle. The coyote is trapped, shot and poisoned because it, too, may occasionally kill a lamb. Study shows, however, that one-third of the coyote's food consists of dead animal remains. When it is caught eating a sheep that was already dead, a coyote is often blamed for something it has not done. The bulk of its food—almost half—is composed of rabbits and rodents. It sometimes eats birds, and it eats some insects and plants also.

It does not make too much sense to kill the coyotes that eat rodents we want to get rid of. We need to study different kinds of wildlife in relation to other kinds if we are to learn anything about their real place in nature, and their relationship to man.

The wolf is rare now in the United States

Dust Bowl

In the early 1930s great clouds of dust began blowing off the land in the central United States. The clouds spread as far as the Atlantic coast, and sometimes out to sea. In 1934 the Capitol at Washington was darkened by the dust clouds. Desks in the skyscraper offices of New York City were covered with dust from our wheat farms in the Great Plains.

Some of the storms covered as many as 300,000 square miles. They carried up to 300 million tons of dried-out soil. Some of them drove great flocks of birds before them. The strong-winged ducks and geese got away, but smaller birds were caught. People's homes and machinery were buried in sand. Airplanes had to fly high, and cars could scarcely move on the highways.

We called the area from northern Texas to the Dakotas the Dust Bowl. The land had been plowed up, and the soil was dried out. Strong winds did the rest. This happened over thousands of square miles, all at the same time. People went broke or moved out, and the land they left was no place for wildlife.

We have learned to keep the soil protected so the winds cannot blow the top soil off. Some of this land needs grass on it. Some needs a cover of mulches. Some needs to be kept in rough, cloddy condition when it has to be plowed. When we keep the soil in place the land benefits, people can live there and there is a home for wildlife as well.

Dust storms make the land unfit either for people or wildlife

Forests and woodlands

A good forest or woodland has many values. It produces lumber, pulp, fuel, turpentine, poles and many other wood products. It provides one of the best protective coverings for land that we know. The canopy of leaves and branches overhead breaks the force of the rain. The mat of rotting leaves and twigs of the forest floor soaks up rainwater like a sponge. There is practically no soil erosion in forests. The water seeps into the ground slowly, instead of dashing off to make floods.

A forest in good condition makes homes for many types of wildlife. A host of warblers and other insect-eating birds live in tall trees. Squirrels and chipmunks, owls, woodpeckers and thrushes live within it. Grouse may drum on fallen logs. Raccoons use it, as do opossums, skunks and woodchucks. In big woods, deer, bear, elk, wildcats and other animals range through the timber. Some animals are seldom found anywhere else.

A third of American land is covered by forest. This is 759 million acres. Of this, two-thirds, or 509 million acres, are what is termed commercial forest land. From this we harvest our timber and other forest products. Our national forests have about 97 million acres of commercial forest. Nearly three-fourths of our commercial forests are privately owned—by farmers, big timber companies and others.

Given good management and protection from fire, all this forest land is of immense value to our wildlife.

Mixed hardwoods and shrubs in this eastern forest provide a variety of habitats for wildlife

Black bear, denizen of forests

Forest fires

All the values of a forest or woodland are ruined by fire. The timber is burned, and vast quantities of fine lumber are lost this way. The water-holding duff of rotting leaves and twigs on the forest floor is destroyed. The wild animals that escape a great fire may not return for many years. With the canopy of leaves and the spongy duff gone, the land erodes as soon as hard rains come. Young seedlings—the future forest—are destroyed and may not grow again for many years. One of the cardinal rules of good forestry is "Prevent forest fires."

Despite all our efforts, some 3 or 4 million acres of forest are destroyed in forest fires every year. It used to be that 10 or 15 million acres were burned, but this number has been reduced. It costs us about 160 million dollars a year, though, to keep the figures as low as they are.

The cigarettes of careless travelers and the campfires of thoughtless campers start many fires. These can be prevented. Fires started by lightning, of course, cannot. But everyone who uses a forest, for camping, hiking or just "passing through" on a road, can help by being extra careful with fire.

Wildlife habitats in a woodland or forest cannot be replaced for perhaps a generation, although fire can destroy them in a day or two. To prevent fires is a good wildlife management rule as well as a good forestry rule.

When timber burns, bears and other forest wildlife suffer

Selective cutting

We know a lot in America about cutting trees. Our forefathers learned because they had to clear the land. We have always had a great deal of timber. Our methods of cutting it are well developed, and we have shipped timber all over the world.

But today our supply of virgin timber is very small compared to what it once was. Lumber costs more. So does paper and other things made from wood.

What we are learning now is not so much *how* to cut, but *when* and *where* to cut, so that we do not destroy the forest when we take out the timber. We are learning that it is wiser to cut only the trees that are ripe. This is what foresters call selective cutting. This means that we carefully select the biggest and best trees that are no longer growing rapidly, and cut these. All the younger trees, that are still growing rapidly and putting on more wood, we leave. Later, when they are mature, we will cut them.

Selective cutting means that the woods are always full of young trees growing up to make timber. In turn, this means that we will always have our woodlands, and that the land they cover will be safe from erosion. It will preserve woodland wildlife also.

Woods with all the trees the same age, and without a good second story of shrubs and young trees, do not have a great many wild creatures in them. Selective cutting is of great value for wildlife. With a good mixture of young and old trees, and with a good understory of shrubs and occasional openings, there are more places for wildlife.

Selective cutting helps woodland wildlife like the ruffed grouse

Den trees

A den tree is one with a hollow place in it where wild creatures find shelter. Raccoons sleep over winter in den trees. Bats and opossums spend their days in them, to come out at night and feed on insects. Honeybees live in them. Woodpeckers, big and little, nest in them. So do flying squirrels. Owls live in them. A forest without den trees has few such creatures.

We used to believe that saving den trees was not good forestry. They take up a lot of space that could be used by young timber trees. They were called "wolf trees" because they ate up so much space.

And yet, curiously enough, in European countries where forestry has been practiced much longer than in America, foresters have another idea. Where their planted forests were clean and park-like, the trees did not do so well. There was no place for wildlife—no underbrush, no den trees, almost no protection at all. Insect pests damaged the trees. Beetles ate holes in the wood. Mice and other rodents gnawed at the roots.

And so, in Europe, the foresters began to put birdhouses in the woods. This seems remarkable, almost foolish. But the birds began to come into the woods and use the boxes. Owls took up quarters in them and fed on the mice. Woodpeckers built their nests in them and fed on the wood-boring insects. Smaller insect-eating birds came too and fed on the pests that were injuring the tree foliage.

We now believe that it is good forestry to leave a few den trees in every acre of forest.

A raccoon looks out of his den in an old maple tree

Woodland edge

Woodland margins are always interesting places to look for wildlife creatures. You will almost always find many more birds there, and many more kinds as well. Biologists have learned that there is about twice as much wildlife along a woodland edge as there is in the woods, or in the field adjacent.

Shrubs along woodland borders offer excellent wildlife shelter for nesting and resting, for escape and even for play. Some of the shrubs, such as dogwoods, hazels, wild cherries, plums, snowberries and sumacs provide food as well.

When the shrub borders are well developed, they have other uses too. For one thing, a thick border growth crowds against the outer row of trees. This causes the trees to lose their lower branches and produce better timber, free of knots. Besides this, good borders prevent strong winds from blowing through the woods. These winds would otherwise dry out and even blow away the litter of leaves and twigs on the ground. Since this layer of duff is so important in holding water and preventing erosion, it is necessary to stop the wind.

Wildlife in the woodland edge can help the farmer who is trying to manage his land properly. Some of the wild creatures that destroy harmful insects in the woods inhabit the woodland edge. So do birds that work over the fields to help prevent trouble with crop pests. The wise farmer protects the woodland margin, and he often plants shrubs there that are most attractive to wildlife.

A good woodland border, useful to the forest and to wildlife such as these wood thrushes

Game farms and food patches

One of the things we have learned about wildlife is that we cannot have more of it than the habitat will support. We must learn what kind of home each type of wildlife needs, then see if we can provide that home. Because we have learned this, there is less interest in game farms and food patches than there used to be.

In some places people still raise game birds from eggs, as we raise chickens. When the birds are grown they are let loose in open fields or woods. The picture shows a pheasant farm.

Pen-raising does not necessarily result in more birds to shoot, because wildlife cannot survive where there is not the kind of food, cover, water and natural protection from enemies that it needs. Or there may already be as many birds in an area as it can support.

Fish, like game birds, are often raised in hatcheries, to be released in lakes, streams and even the oceans. Most biologists, however, say we can get better fishing by more careful management of wild fish that grow up in our lakes and streams.

In order to grow food for wildlife, people sometimes plant food patches. A food patch may be sown to corn, wheat, sunflower, sorghum or other cultivated crops. Food patches are expensive because they usually consist of annual crops that must be planted each spring. They also take up good cropland. They are most useful where the primary use of the land is for hunting.

Ring-necked pheasants on a game farm

Wildlife in the suburbs

Many millions of Americans live on the edges of cities, in the suburbs. They are more or less halfway between the city and the country. Many birds and other animals may live in their community and are a lot of fun to watch.

A good bird feeder is one way to attract the birds. You can get one at the nearest hardware store, or build one of your own. Set it up near a window so that you can watch what goes on. You should feed birds the year round for best results. Your best buys for feed are sunflower seeds, cracked corn and peanut butter. Most pet stores carry the seeds and corn.

Feeding table scraps to attract raccoons or foxes or squirrels—depending on where you live—is exciting too. The squirrels feed during the day, the foxes and 'coons at night. You may want to set up a floodlight to help you watch. It may take a long time before you get the animals coming—but they'll come.

No one knows how many millions of feeders are in operation in this country, but the number is very large. This is the way the suburbanite can get to see, close up, a wide variety of birds and mammals. It also helps to keep the populations of wildlife well fed.

Bird baths and birdhouses are useful too, in attracting birds. So also are plenty of berry-bearing shrubs plus evergreens for cover. You can experiment with various kinds of feeders. With a pair of binoculars and a good bird book, anyone can learn a lot about American wildlife.

A house for purple martins is always popular

Wildlife's place

Wildlife is economically important. We have learned that it provides a large fur harvest in the United States, and that our fisheries are worth millions of dollars each year. Much of the annual bill for sporting goods in this country is for hunting and fishing equipment. Many guides make their living from hunting and fishing parties.

Wildlife contributes immeasurably to American recreation. When we hunt and fish or visit our great out-of-doors we get away from city life and obtain needed relaxation and enjoyment. Taking photographs of wildlife is a hobby for many people.

Wild creatures have an important beauty or aesthetic value. Native animals have been the inspiration for magnificent statues, paintings and stories. We use them for patterns in cloth, furniture and architecture. We thrill to the sight of a soaring eagle or a running antelope, and enjoy the songs and bright colors of our native birds.

Wild animals have an ecological value—they help to keep a natural balance in the living world. Birds and small mammals eat weed seeds. When harmful beetles or moths occur in large numbers, wild birds and mammals help to reduce them. When we are not careful to protect wildlife, we may suffer for it.

Wildlife takes its place along with forests, grasslands, waters and soil as a part of the great American heritage of natural resources. If we are to remain a great nation we shall have to see to it that these resources are used well, so that they may be with us forever.

Wildlife is a natural resource of great importance to a nation

Land pattern

The homes for wildlife in America depend upon the way we use the land. In the United States today we are cultivating nearly 400 million acres of land and, if we need to, we can cultivate 25 million acres more. There are 400 million acres of forests, and even more than that of western rangeland. Most of America's 1,900 million acres are used for something—crops, timber, livestock. Wildlife must find its home on these lands. The way we use the land determines to a large extent the kind of place we make for wildlife.

Where we treat the land well, wildlife almost always finds a good home. On eroded, badly used land wildlife finds poor shelter and little food. Many of the things described in this book—ponds, borders, strip cropping, hedges, vegetated streambanks, good pastures, protected woods—help us to use the land wisely. They also make first-rate homes for wildlife.

On millions of farms and ranches from one end of the country to the other, the land pattern is changing. Square fields that did not fit the land are giving way to fields that follow the contour. Crops are planted in strips that fit the land. Steep slopes that eroded are being covered now with pasture grasses, or planted to trees to conserve the soil and use the land most wisely.

We are learning to use the land more carefully in America. As the new land pattern takes shape we protect the soil that is the source of our food and the foundation of our nation's welfare. The same pattern provides more homes for wildlife, so that it too may be preserved.

As the new pattern of conservation spreads,
America will become a better place for wildlife

Further reading

Allen, Durward. Our Wildlife Legacy. New York: Funk & Wagnalls, 1964

Bodsworth, Fred. The Last of the Curlews. New York: Dodd, Mead & Co., 1955

Cahalane, Victor. Mammals of America. New York: The Macmillan Company, 1947

Carson, Rachel. Silent Spring. Boston, Mass.: Houghton Mifflin Company, 1962

______. The Sea Around Us (revised edition). New York: Oxford University Press, Inc., 1961

Dassman, Raymond F. Wildlife Biology. New York: John Wiley & Sons, Inc., 1964

Davison, Verne E. Attracting Birds: from the Prairies to the Atlantic. New York: Thomas Y. Crowell Company, 1967

Graham, Edward H. Natural Principles of Land Use. New York: Oxford University Press, Inc., 1944

Griffin, Donald R. Bird Migration. New York: Doubleday & Company, Inc., 1964

Leopold, Aldo. Sand County Almanac (revised edition). New York: Oxford University Press, Inc., 1966

Life Nature Library. New York: Time-Life Books

Matthiessen, Peter. Wildlife in America. New York: The Viking Press, Inc., 1964

Seton, Ernest Thompson. Lives of Game Animals. Newton Centre, Mass.: Charles T. Branford Co., originally published 1925

Write for lists of available publications on wildlife to:

U.S. Fish and Wildlife Service, Washington, D.C. 20242

National Audubon Society, 1130 Fifth Avenue, New York, N.Y. 10028

U.S. Conservation Service, Washington, D.C. 20250

State Game, Fish or Conservation Department or Commission at your state capital

To help you identify wildlife, try:

The Golden Guides. New York: Golden Press

Field Guide series. Boston, Mass.: Houghton Mifflin Company

Putnam's Nature Field Books. New York: G.P. Putnam's Sons

Sources of Illustration

Francis L. Jaques page 55
National Audubon Society pages 67, 75, 83
National Park Service pages 11, 89 (top), 129
Penna Game Commission page 65
U.S. Department of the Interior, Fish and Wildlife Service pages 13 (bottom), 15, 17, 29, 35, 37, 39, 41, 43, 45, 47, 49, 51, 59 (bottom), 69, 73, 77, 81, 85, 141 (bottom), 143
U.S. Forest Service pages 19, 21, 31, 33, 71, 127 (bottom), 133 (bottom), 135 (bottom), 139
USDA, Soil Conservation Service pages 13 (top), 23, 25, 57, 59 (top), 61, 63, 87, 89 (bottom), 91, 93, 97, 99, 101, 103, 105, 107 (top and bottom), 109, 111 (top and bottom), 113 (top and bottom), 115 (top and bottom), 117, 119, 121 (top and bottom), 123, 125 (top and bottom), 127 (top), 131, 133 (top), 135 (top), 137 (top and bottom), 141 (top), 145, 147, 149

Index

Italic numbers indicate illustrations.